Handbook
of
Needlepoint
Stitches

Handbook of Needlepoint Stitches

***

Mary Meister Walzer

VNR VAN NOSTRAND REINHOLD COMPANY
NEW YORK CINCINNATI TORONTO LONDON MELBOURNE

*I dedicate this book to all my friends and students, without
whose help I never would have been able to write this book.*

ACKNOWLEDGMENTS

A special thanks to Carole Widder, who did all the stitch
examples so excellently; to Louise Siegel, who gave me
my first encouragement; and to Barbara Klinger, my
editor, who tied everything together so well.

Van Nostrand Reinhold Company Regional Offices:
New York Cincinnati Chicago Millbrae Dallas
Van Nostrand Reinhold Company International Offices:
London Toronto Melbourne
Library of Congress Catalog Card Number 70-153457

Designed by Myron Hall III
Diagrams by Mary Meister Walzer
All photographs by Fred Picker (except page 25, left, by Barbara Klinger)
Printed and bound in Tokyo, Japan, by Toppan Printing Co., Ltd.
Published in 1971 by Van Nostrand Reinhold Company,
a Division of Litton Educational Publishing, Inc.
450 West 33rd Street, New York, N.Y. 10001
Published simultaneously in Canada by
Van Nostrand Reinhold Ltd.
16 15 14 13 12 11 10 9 8 7 6 5 4 3

Contents

INTRODUCTION

The term needlepoint was previously applied only to canvas work done either in short, slanted stitches known as Tent Stitches (The Continental and the Basket Weave are both Tent Stitches) or in the common Half Cross Stitch. However, all stitchery done on canvas has now come to be known as needlepoint, and there are many varieties of stitches besides the Tent and the Half Cross that are used in this work. This book will describe and diagram the most important ones and enable the reader to use a broad range of stitches in creating needlepoint.

Before going on to the stitches you should become familiar with the materials you will be using. The canvas on which the stitches are worked is a mesh fabric woven of evenly spaced vertical and horizontal threads. There are two different types of canvas. Mono-canvas is woven with single threads in both directions to form the mesh. Penelope canvas is woven with double threads in both directions. The gauge of the canvas is measured by the number of mesh, or openings between the the threads, per inch. Canvas with 5 mesh per inch is always woven with double threads; so wherever 5-mesh canvas is mentioned in this book you will know it is penelope. Canvas with 10 mesh or more per inch can be either penelope or mono-canvas. In this book, 10-mesh canvas always refers to mono-canvas unless otherwise stated. Canvas is sold by the yard and is available at needlework shops and at large department stores.

As in other needlework, the stitches are made by moving the needle in and out of the fabric. In this case, the needle moves in and out of the mesh openings so that the yarn covers the threads of the canvas. To cover the threads well, you must use the proper yarn or wool. I have found that the best wool to use for most stitches is Persian wool. This comes in lengths made up of three strands. When directions call for three strands of wool, use the wool just as it comes. When the directions call for six strands, use two lengths together. The lengths can easily be split into single strands and threaded into the needle separately when the directions call for one, two, four or five strands of wool. Colbert 6 wool can be used in place of Persian wool. You can also experiment with silk, cotton, metallic thread and other yarns for unusual effects once you have become proficient with wool.

If you buy wool by the yard instead of in ready-cut lengths, cut it into a manageable size before you thread the needle. The maximum length you should work with is about 24 inches. On large mesh canvas you may have to use rug wool instead of Persian wool.

The appropriate size of the needle you will need depends on the mesh size of the canvas, since the needle must be able to fit through the openings in the canvas. Use a #18 tapestry needle on 10-mesh canvas and a #20 tapestry needle on 14-mesh canvas. On 5-mesh canvas, use a large yarn needle.

To start a piece of work, always tape the edges of the canvas with masking tape so that they do not unravel. Do not knot your wool. Leave a 1-inch tail of wool on the back of the canvas when you bring your needle through the mesh to begin your stitch. This tail should be worked into the back of the first three or four stitches on the completed row. After the work is in progress, pull each new length of wool through the back of three or four completed stitches to start it and

Lengths of Persian wool are made up of three strands, which can be used together or split into separate units.

Canvas that measures 5 mesh to the inch is always woven with double threads in both directions.

Mono-canvas is woven with single threads in both directions. This 10-mesh mono-canvas is standard for needlepoint.

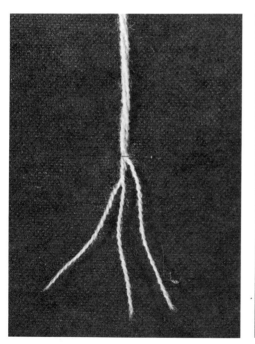

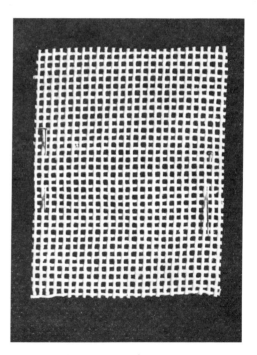

to finish it. Do not leave any long ends hanging.

The stitches you select to work your design will depend on the effect you want to achieve. Some stitches have more texture than others; some are more elaborate and provide strong design elements of their own; some are more appropriate than others for background areas. As you look at the examples in this book and actually work the different stitches, you will discover which ones are best suited for a specific effect and which ones can be combined attractively. You will find that the choice of stitches is just as important as the design itself. Some crewel stitches can also be used to enhance your work.

The design can be anything from pictorial representation to geometric patterns. Always plan to work your canvas 1-inch larger all around than the desired size of the finished piece so that none of the design will be lost in finishing off the edges.

The first step in putting your design on canvas is to draw it on a piece of paper in black ink. Place the drawing on a table or board and lay the piece of canvas over it. Tack down both to the table or board with push pins. Use a soft-lead (2B or 3B) art pencil

and trace the design on the canvas, making sure it is centered. Where a straight line is indicated, run your pencil along the nearest line of mesh threads.

If you wish to paint your design on the canvas, you can use oil-base markers (I find Eagle one of the best) or the new acrylic paints. Usually only an outline of the design is necessary, but you can color in the entire design if you wish. Always test the marker or paint for colorfastness first by putting some on a small piece of canvas. Let it dry and then embroider over it in a light color wool. Dip this piece of canvas in cold water and allow it to dry. If the marker or paint does not run, then you know it is safe to use.

If you want to reduce or enlarge a design you have found, you can usually do so by ruling a grid of squares over it and transferring each line of the design within a square to a piece of graph paper according to the scale you desire. You can also take the original artwork to a photo-enlarger and have a copy of it reproduced in the exact size you want.

When you have completed the design and finished working the stitches, you will have to block the canvas to eliminate or minimize

any distortion caused by the wool pulling against the canvas threads. First sew around the edges of the canvas with a sewing machine to prevent unraveling. Then dip the canvas into cold water to which you have added a drop of Woolite. Roll the canvas work in a towel to remove excess moisture. Take any piece of board and cover it with aluminum foil. Tack the canvas work face up to the board with thumbtacks. Begin at one side of the canvas and work around all the edges, pulling the canvas tight and straight as you go. When the canvas work is thoroughly dry, untack it and remove it from the board.

The practical applications of canvas work are manifold. Wall hangings, upholstery fabrics, rugs and pillow covers are a few of the items you can fashion from canvas work. (Be sure to consult an upholsterer for the correct size of the fabric required before you work the canvas.) Here are some simple directions for adding the finishing touches to wall hangings, rugs, and pillow covers.

If you wish to use the finished canvas work as a wall panel, block it by tacking it directly to a canvas stretcher while it is wet. You can purchase a canvas stretcher in a

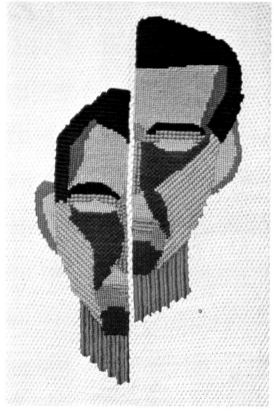

Mural designed by the author and worked by Rhoda Rothman. Done in Byzantine, Diagonal Cashmere, Diagonal Mosaic, Bargello, French Knots, Smyrna Cross, Milanese, Horizontal Cashmere, Rice, Continental, and Horizontal Scotch Stitches.

Wall panel designed by the author and worked by Frances Aronoff. Done in Gobelin, Diagonal Mosaic, Cross, Smyrna Cross, Rice, Stem, Continental, and Brick Stitches.

9

Above: Wall panel designed and worked by the author. Done in Brick, Horizontal Mosaic, Diagonal Cashmere, Diagonal Mosaic, and Continental Stitches.

Right: Op art Bargello worked as a wall hanging by the author.

Sampler by Rhoda Rothman includes: Bargello, Byzantine, Scotch, Gobelin, Smyrna Cross, Rice, Algerian Eye, Brick, Diagonal Mosaic, Diagonal and Horizontal Cashmere, Plaited Gobelin, Encroaching Oblique, Double Leviathan, Triple Leviathan, Triangle, Leaf, Rococo, Web, Milanese, Kalem, and Continental Stitches.

Bargello pillow designed by the author and worked by Judy Walzer in three colors.

Bargello belt by Carole Widder. Laced and lined in leather.

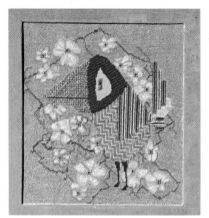

Top left: Wall hanging designed by the author and worked by Joan Wallach. Birds and flowers done in Cross and Continental Stitches with Brick Stitch background.

Top right: Bird designed and worked by the author. Done in Diagonal Mosaic, Stem, Byzantine, Algerian Eye, Cross, and Tent Stitches.

Bottom left: Parrot by Jean Kummel. Done in Half Cross and Upright Cross, with Gobelin Stitch and Crewel added for details.

Bottom right: Cardinal by Jean Kummel. Done in Half Cross, Milanese, and Satin Stitches with Gobelin Stitch for border.

suitable size, to the closest inch, in an art store.

Hangings look pretty suspended from a dowel with wool loops. Either a macramé or a plain fringe trimming can be added to the bottom of the finished canvas piece.

To make a plain fringe for a rug, pillow, or hanging, cut your wool into pieces 6 inches long. Insert a crochet hook into the edge of your work. Catch the middle of the wool with the hook and pull it through the canvas, making a loop. Draw each of the two loose ends of wool through the loop and pull them down tightly. Trim the fringe to the desired length when finished.

To cover a standard-sized pillow (12″ x 12″, 14″ x 14″, 16″ x 16″) with a needleworked design, turn the finished canvas piece inside out and sew it to a fabric backing with seams on three edges. Turn the cover right side out. Put the pillow inside and sew the fourth side together with a blind hemstitch.

There are many other items you can make by using your own ingenuity. You can turn your canvas work into belts, bags, and other fashion accessories by consulting specialty firms that furnish the necessary hardware and finishings.

If you follow the numbers carefully on the diagrams that follow, you should have no trouble creating all of the stitches described in this book.

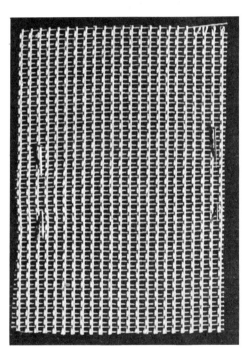

Penelope canvas with 10 mesh to the inch.

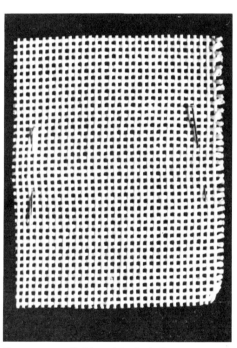

Mono-canvas with 14 mesh to the inch.

CONTINENTAL STITCH

The Continental Stitch is a Tent Stitch and is the most common stitch used on mono-canvas. It is used to fill in details within a small space, to outline shapes, and to make narrow, straight lines. It is also good for a simple background. Follow Diagram A. Always stitch from right to left, working horizontal rows of stitches across the canvas. Turn the canvas upside down for each new row, keeping the needle and yarn on the wrong side of the canvas until you begin the new row. Use three strands of wool on 10-mesh canvas. Diagram B shows the position of the needle while working.

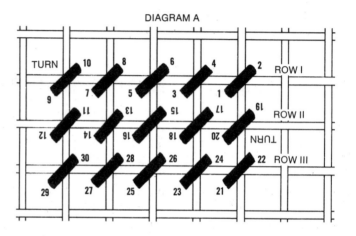

DIAGRAM A

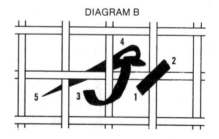

DIAGRAM B

Continental Stitch, front of canvas.

Continental Stitch, rear of canvas.

BASKET WEAVE STITCH

Another Tent Stitch, Basket Weave is used when a small stitch is needed to work solid areas. It is very good for shading in areas on flowers and faces. The Basket Weave looks like the Continental but is much stronger because of its firm construction, which is evident when viewed from the back of the canvas. It is better for large areas because it does not pull the canvas out of shape.

Follow Diagram A for the steps. Work the stitches in diagonal rows up and down the canvas. It is not necessary to turn the canvas upside down unless you have to fill in vacant canvas in the other side of the design. Use three strands of wool on 10-mesh canvas. Begin the first row at the lower right corner of the canvas.

Note the position of the needle in various stages. Diagram B shows the needle is always parallel to the horizontal threads of the canvas when the diagonal row is moving upward. Diagram C shows the needle is parallel to the vertical threads when the row is moving down the canvas. The only time the needle is in a diagonal position under the canvas threads is to begin the first stitch of a new row, either moving up the canvas or down it. In the diagram, these stitches are 7-8, 13-14 and 19-20.

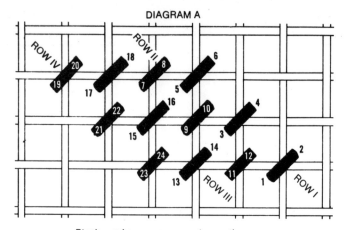

DIAGRAM A

Black numbers = rows moving up the canvas

White numbers = rows moving down the canvas

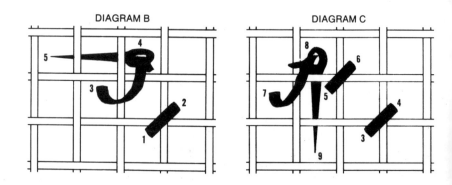

DIAGRAM B

DIAGRAM C

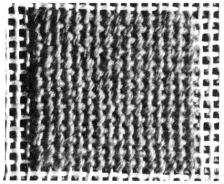

Basket Weave Stitch resembles Continental when seen from front of canvas.

Rear of canvas shows construction of Basket Weave is firmer than that of Continental Stitch.

Shaded flower designed by the author in Basket Weave Tent Stitch. Can be used as a repeat pattern or enlarged.

HALF CROSS STITCH

The Half Cross Stitch is another short, slanted stitch, but it can be done only on penelope canvas and is used there instead of the Continental Stitch. It looks like the Continental but uses much less wool, provides a weaker backing, and is worked from left to right. The canvas must be turned upside down for each new row. Use three strands of wool on 10-mesh canvas and heavy rug wool on 5-mesh canvas. Six strands of Persian wool will cover 5-mesh if the canvas is painted the same color as the wool.

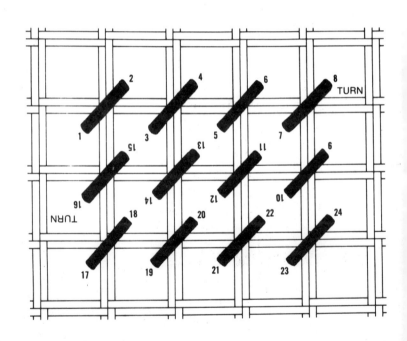

Wall panel designed by author and worked by Joan Wallach. Background is done in Half Cross and flowers are done in Cross Stitches on 5-mesh canvas. The Cross Stitch is based on the Half Cross but gives a more raised effect.

Half Cross Stitch on penelope canvas.

CROSS STITCH (Penelope Canvas)

The Cross Stitch here can only be done on penelope canvas. On 10-mesh penelope canvas, you use three strands of wool. On 5-mesh penelope canvas, the stitch looks best in six strands of wool. This is a very good rug stitch and can also be done in rug wool on 3-mesh canvas. Work a row of Half Cross Stitches in one direction and cross the stitches by returning along the row in the opposite direction as in the diagram. All the top stitches must slant in the same direction; therefore all the rows must begin at the left and be worked back over from the right.
If rows are begun at the right, they must be worked back over from the left.

CROSS STITCH (Mono-Canvas)

On mono-canvas, the Cross Stitch must be worked with the stitches slanted over two horizontal and two vertical threads of canvas. The canvas does not have to be turned. You go across the row with the stitches slanted in one direction and add the top stitches by working back along the same row in the opposite direction. Because you are working over more threads, you need four or five strands of wool to cover 10-mesh mono-canvas. The Cross Stitch is good to use in small designs and makes a nice textured line.

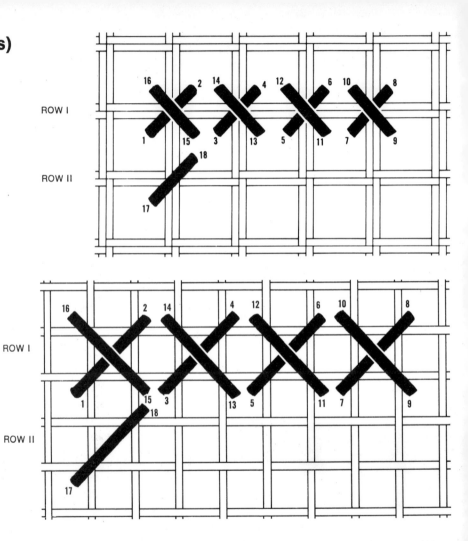

20

Rug by Louise Siegel. Cross Stitch with fringe, worked on penelope canvas.

Cross Stitch (Penelope Canvas)

Cross Stitch (Mono-Canvas)

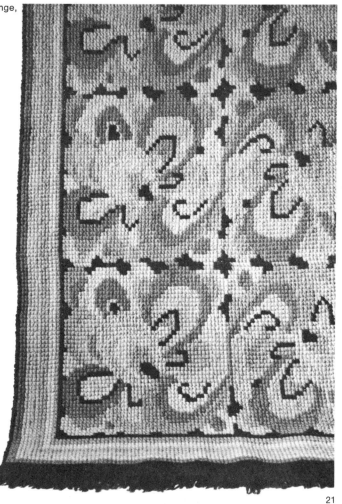

UPRIGHT CROSS STITCH

The Upright Cross is done in three strands of wool on 10-mesh canvas or in rug wool on 5-mesh canvas. It is best for small areas as it works up very slowly. Each cross is completed separately. The vertical stitch is made first and the horizontal stitch is placed across it. The alternate rows can be done in a different color. The stitch can be worked from left to right, as in Rows I and III, or from right to left as in Row II.

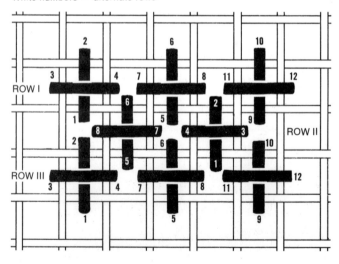

White numbers = alternate rows

Upright Cross Stitch

Wall panel by Jean Kummel. Parrot done in Upright
Cross and Half Cross Stitches, with Gobelin Stitches
for outlining and Crewel Stitches added to the eye.
Note that the Upright Cross Stitches have a slightly
raised appearance.

SMYRNA CROSS STITCH

The Smyrna Cross is actually a regular Cross Stitch with an Upright Cross Stitch on top of it. Put all regular Cross Stitches in first, using three strands of wool on 10-mesh canvas. Steps are shown by numbers. For the top crosses, follow the letters (A-P) and use a single strand of another color wool. This stitch fits nicely into small areas and looks good in flowers, leaves, and stems.

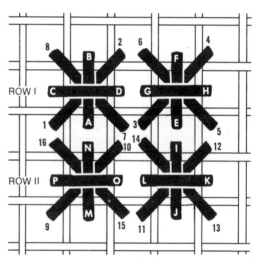

Black numbers = Cross Stitch

White letters = Upright Cross Stitch

24

Smyrna Cross Stitch

Designed by author, worked by Ruth Greer. Cross
Stitches are combined with Smyrna Cross Stitches
(worked in two colors) against a background of
Tent Stitches. Can be used as a repeat pattern.

TRAMÉ CROSS STITCH

Tramé Cross Stitch on 10-mesh canvas is a
nice, small stitch that is useful as a filler or for
a textured line. It is especially pretty done in
two colors. First put in the long, horizontal
threads, using three strands of wool. This is the
tramé and is designated by letters in the
diagram. Do each row unevenly as shown. Add
the Cross Stitches on top of the tramé, using
one or two strands of wool so that the tramé
color shows through. Follow the numbers in the
diagram for the Cross Stitches.

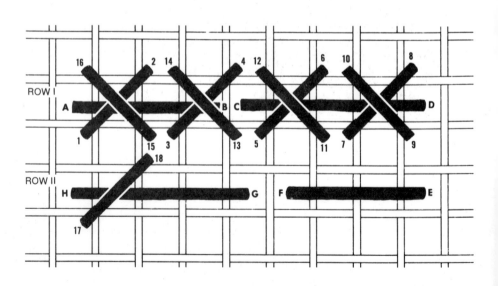

Tramé Cross Stitch

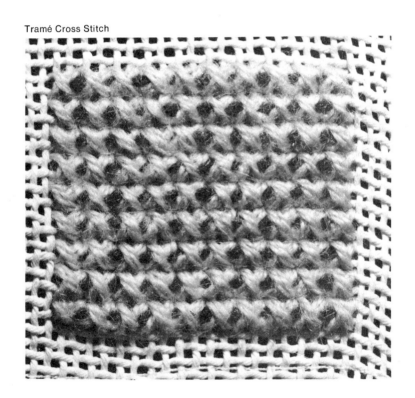

RICE STITCH

The Rice Stitch is a Cross Stitch with a diagonal top stitch added to each corner. It is not as complicated to do as it looks if you work symmetrically. Put all Cross Stitches in first, following the numbers and using the same method as for a regular Cross Stitch on mono-canvas. Then add the top stitches in another color, following the letters in order from A to P (black letters). At the end of the row, turn the canvas upside down to repeat steps A to P (white letters) on the following row.

This stitch looks good worked as shown in the diagram using 5-mesh penelope canvas with six strands of wool for the Cross Stitches and three strands of another color for the top stitches. If you work this stitch on 10-mesh mono-canvas, use three strands of wool for the Cross Stitches and one strand for the top stitches and try to use it in small areas as it is very time consuming on that size canvas.

Turn for white letters

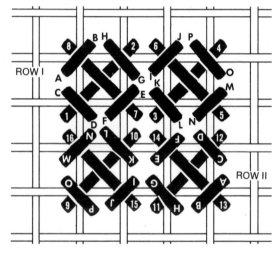

28

Design by Carole Widder. Rice Stitch in two colors
on 5-mesh canvas.

Rice Stitch

DOUBLE LEVIATHAN STITCH

The Double Leviathan begins with a large Cross Stitch and ends with a large Upright Cross Stitch. Four other diagonal stitches are added in the order given in the diagram. The Double Leviathan is done in three strands of wool on 10-mesh canvas. It makes a beautiful, patterned stitch and a line of backstitches can be added between all the rows for decorative effect and for better coverage. (See page 38 for backstitches.) For a pretty effect, use a different color wool starting with step 13 and use that color for the backstitches. Rows can be worked either horizontally or vertically.

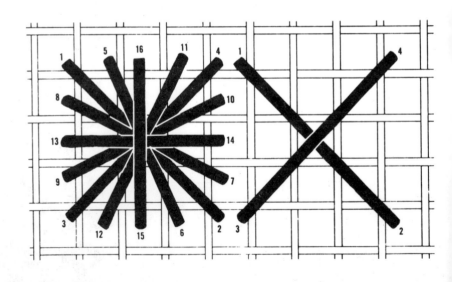

Design by Debbie Cohen. Double Leviathan Stitch in three colors with backstitch between rows.

TRIPLE LEVIATHAN STITCH

The Triple Leviathan Stitch is a series of slanted stitches combined with five Upright Cross Stitches. This Leviathan is done in three strands of wool on 10-mesh canvas. It is a single, decorative stitch and must be worked with another stitch, such as the Continental or Basket Weave, as a background. It is done in two colors.

Diagram A shows the order in which the slanted stitches are made. Follow the sequence, beginning at point 1 and always going back to the center for each new stitch. Use a single color for all twelve stitches. Diagram B shows how to add the Upright Cross Stitches in the second color.

C = Center mesh

DIAGRAM A

DIAGRAM B

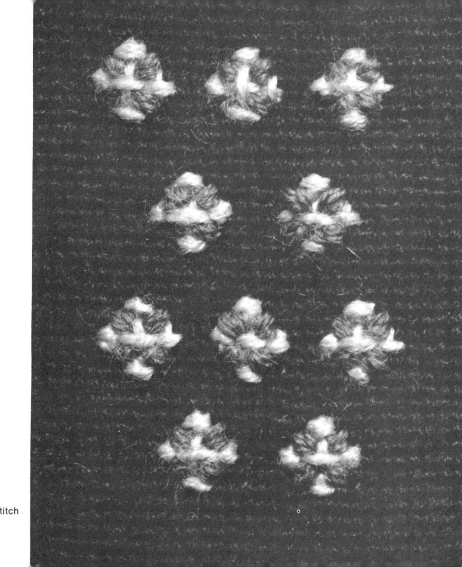

Triple Leviathan Stitch

KNOTTED STITCH

The Knotted Stitch is a long, slanted stitch with a short top stitch crossing it in the opposite direction. It is worked with three strands of wool on 10-mesh canvas. Each slanted stitch is crossed before the next one is made. The canvas does not have to be turned and the stitch can be worked back and forth in horizontal rows. This stitch fits into small areas where a textured effect is needed. It is rather slow to work up.

Knotted Stitch

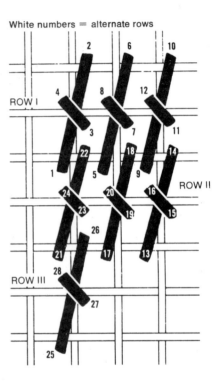

White numbers = alternate rows

34

ROCOCO STITCH

The Rococo Stitch is a series of four vertical stitches held down in a diamond shape by four short, top stitches. It makes a good design when worked in six strands of wool on 5-mesh penelope canvas; you can arrange the individual diamond-shapes to form different patterns as in the photograph. Do not pull the vertical stitches too taut or you will not be able to tie them in place. The Rococo can also be done in three strands of wool on 10-mesh canvas.

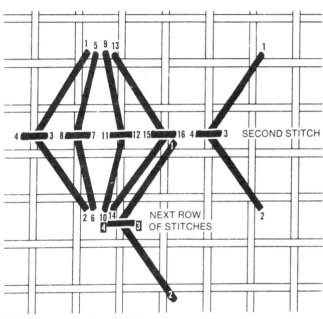

White numbers = alternate rows

Designed by author and worked by Ruth Greer on 5-mesh canvas in Rococo Stitch. Individual Rococo Stitches are arranged in groups of four to form large diamonds alternating in color.

WEB STITCH

The Web Stitch consists of diagonal stitches
held down by small top stitches. It is done
in two strands of wool on 10-mesh canvas. This
stitch is good where a triangle is needed. It
gives a nice woven effect, but it works up too
slowly to be used as a background stitch.
Work it in the numerical sequence given, tying
down each diagonal as you go. If you wish
to do the top stitches in another color, you can
use two needles, starting the second color and
needle at stitch 1-2 and proceeding to
stitch 5-6 after you have put in the first diagonal
stitch (3-4) with the other needle and color.

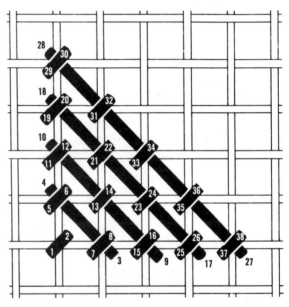

Black numbers = diagonal stitches
White numbers = top stitches

Web Stitch

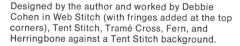

Designed by the author and worked by Debbie Cohen in Web Stitch (with fringes added at the top corners), Tent Stitch, Tramé Cross, Fern, and Herringbone against a Tent Stitch background.

SLANTING GOBELIN STITCH

The Slanting Gobelin Stitch is one of many larger, slanted or oblique stitches that are used to produce different effects than those provided by the short, slanted Tent Stitches. This stitch gives a nice ribbed effect. It can be worked over from two to five horizontal threads of canvas (Tent Stitches are worked over òne thread). I prefer to work this Gobelin over two threads with three strands of wool on 10-mesh canvas, with backstitches between horizontal rows. It can also be worked without a backstitch, but you should then use four or five strands of wool instead of three to cover the canvas better.

Slanting Gobelin is good either as a ribbed filler or for an entire background; it can also be used where a straight line is needed. Diagram A shows that the stitch is worked in horizontal rows from left to right. (If you wish to work the Gobelin slanted in the opposite direction, work each row from right to left but keep the same needle movements.) Turn the canvas upside down for each new row. After the rows are finished, put backstitches in between them in two strands of a different color wool. The letters show the stitching sequence for backstitches.

Diagram B shows that the position of the needle is vertical when going under the canvas threads.

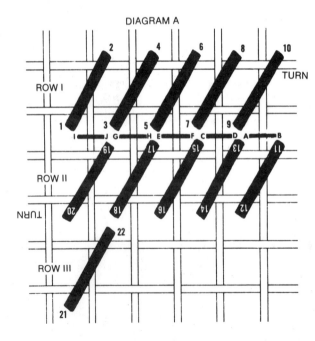

DIAGRAM A

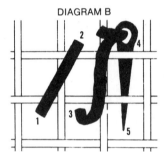

DIAGRAM B

White numbers = alternate rows

38

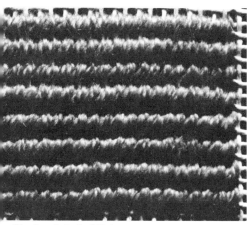

Slanting Gobelin Stitch

Designed by the author and worked by Ruth Greer.
Squares of Slanting Gobelin with backstitches
between rows alternate with rectangles done in the
Continental Stitch.

ENCROACHING GOBELIN STITCH

Encroaching Gobelin consists of Slanting Gobelin stitches worked so that an extra row is placed between two regular rows of stitches. This gives a woven appearance instead of a ribbed one. Use three strands of wool on 10-mesh canvas. Work the stitches in the sequence given, turning the canvas upside down for each new row. If you use two colors, work the first one from left to right on Row I. Begin the second color at point 20 on Row II and work to the right. Work each color back on their alternate rows from left to right with canvas turned upside down. The Encroaching Gobelin Stitch makes an excellent background. It can be worked over two horizontal threads as in the photograph or over four horizontal threads as in the diagram, also over three or five threads.

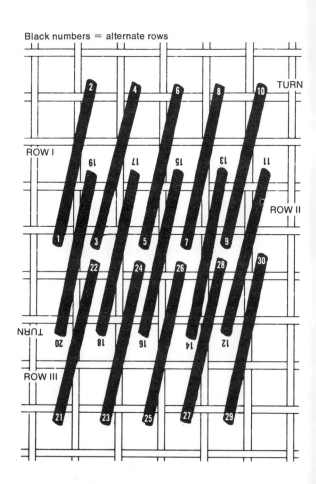

Black numbers = alternate rows

40

Encroaching Gobelin Stitch

OBLIQUE SLAV STITCH

The Oblique Slav Stitch has a greater slant to
it than the Gobelin and covers a wider area
in fewer steps because the stitch is placed
over four vertical threads of canvas. You use
three strands of wool on 10-mesh canvas and
work up and down the canvas in diagonal rows.
You can also work the stitches with the
canvas turned sideways. The Oblique Slav
covers large areas smoothly and quickly and
can also be used to make a single, slanted line.

Oblique Slav Stitch

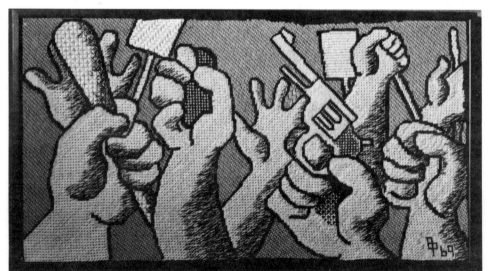

Wall panel by Beth Perrone. Adapted from *Time*
Magazine cover. Shading of arms and hands done
in Oblique Slav. Other areas done in Diagonal
Scotch (slanted in alternate directions), Milanese,
Smyrna Cross, Rice, Gobelin, Continental, and
Diagonal Mosaic Stitches.

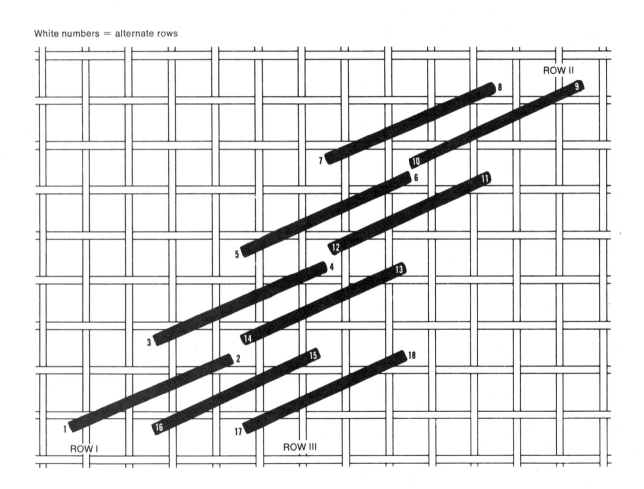

White numbers = alternate rows

ROW II

ROW I

ROW III

43

ENCROACHING OBLIQUE STITCH

The Encroaching Oblique is another long,
slanted stitch. Like the Oblique Slav, it is
worked over four vertical threads of canvas.
However, it is slanted in the opposite direction
and at a sharper angle (each stitch covers
only one horizontal thread instead of two).
Using three strands of wool on 10-mesh canvas,
work the stitch in horizontal rows as in the
diagram, or turn the canvas and the diagram
sideways and work the rows vertically. You must
turn the canvas as well as the diagram in
order to work vertically or the results will
look like the Encroaching Gobelin instead of
the Encroaching Oblique. This stitch makes
a good single line and is excellent for filling in
entire backgrounds or certain design areas
(such as tree trunks) with texture.

Encroaching Oblique Stitch

White numbers = alternate rows worked back in opposite direction

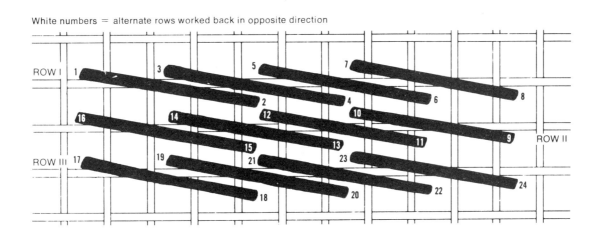

45

HORIZONTAL MOSAIC STITCH

The Horizontal Mosaic Stitch and the eight other stitches that follow are all made by combining long, slanted stitches with short ones. In the Horizontal Mosaic, the basic unit or pattern is one short, one long, and one short stitch forming a square. This pattern is worked in horizontal rows going across the canvas from right to left. Use three strands of wool on 10-mesh canvas.

If you use one color throughout follow the diagram, turning the canvas upside down to begin each new row. Proceed directly from point 24 of the finished row to point 1 of the new row. If you use a second color for the alternate rows, or want to create a striped effect with different colors, start every row at the right as in Row I of the diagram and work without turning the canvas.

For a checkerboard effect, use two needles, each threaded with a different color, and alternate them for each square in the row. This stitch can be used for straight lines as well as for striped or checkerboard effects. Since it takes up little room, it is suitable for small areas as well as large areas.

White numbers = alternate rows

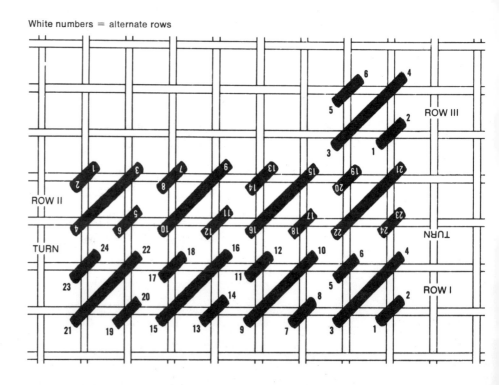

46

Horizontal Mosaic Stitch

Wall panel designed by the author and worked by
Charlotte Schloss. Done in Horizontal Mosaic,
Diagonal Cashmere, Gobelin, Brick, Smyrna Cross
and Continental Stitches. The Gobelin Stitches
forming the lion's mane were worked with the
canvas turned sideways.

DIAGONAL MOSAIC STITCH

The Diagonal Mosaic Stitch is a pattern of alternating short and long stitches worked in diagonal rows. Instead of forming squares like the Horizontal Mosaic, this creates a distinct diagonal stripe. This stitch is appropriate where a strong slant is needed in a narrow space. Using three strands of wool on 10-mesh canvas, begin a row at the bottom right and work toward the upper left of the area you are covering. Turn the canvas for the next row and again work upward from the lower right corner to the upper left.

For this stitch and all other stitches worked in diagonal rows, it is especially important to place your first row across the largest area you plan to fill and work the shorter rows around it. Separate Tent Stitches can be used to fill any vacant spaces left between rows at the outer edges. If you use a second color for the alternate rows, start each color at the bottom and work upward. Use two needles and turn the canvas for every other row.

Designed by author. Petals are in Diagonal Mosaic, Gobelin, Byzantine, and Continental. Leaves are in Smyrna Cross; background is in Brick Stitch. One petal of Diagonal Mosaic was worked with the canvas held upright and another was worked with the canvas held sideways. The Gobelin Stitches were worked slanted toward the upper left corner of the canvas with the rows worked from right to left.

Diagonal Mosaic Stitch

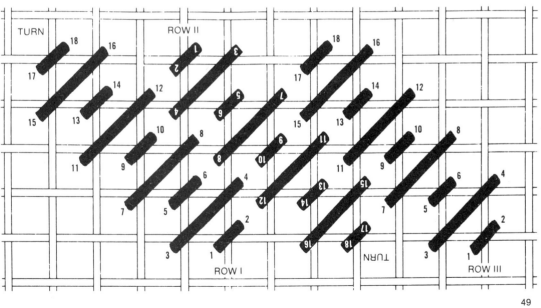

49

HORIZONTAL CASHMERE STITCH

The Horizontal Cashmere has a pattern of one short, two long, and one short stitch. It is very much like the Horizontal Mosaic, but it has an additional long stitch in each series and therefore has a more rectangular effect. It also takes up slightly more room and is less sharply slanted. It is worked from right to left in three strands of wool on 10-mesh canvas.

If you work the rows in one color, turn the canvas for each new row and proceed directly from point 32 of the finished row to point 1 of the next row. For two colors, turn the canvas after you have completed one row of *each* color, starting each at the right as in Row I. Complete the next row of each color by working both as shown in Row II of the diagram. When bringing the needle from point 32 to point 1 for the next row of the same color, skip the space taken by the intervening row of the alternate color. The Horizontal Cashmere is effective to fill in rectangular or square areas.

Designed and worked by Carole Widder in Horizontal Cashmere Stitch. Can be used as a repeat pattern or enlarged.

Horizontal Cashmere Stitch

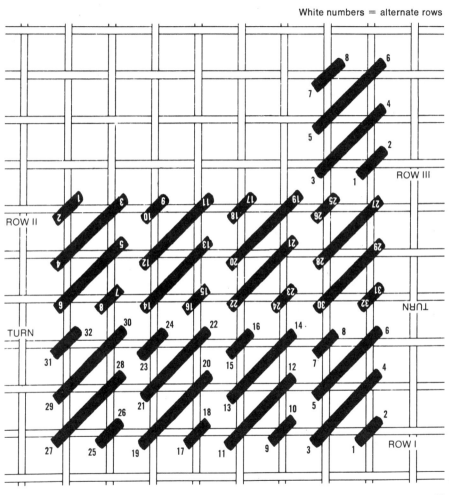

DIAGONAL CASHMERE STITCH

The Diagonal Cashmere has the same series of
stitches (one short, two long, and one short)
as the Horizontal Cashmere, but it is worked in
diagonal rows, resulting in slanted lines.
Rows of Diagonal Cashmere have less of a
slant and cover a larger area than comparable
rows of Diagonal Mosaic. Use three strands
of wool on 10-mesh canvas. Work each row
from the lower right to the upper left, turning the
canvas to begin each new row. Note in the
diagram that, to keep the diagonal pattern, each
short stitch must have a long stitch placed
next to it when the next row is worked. That is
why Row II starts with a long stitch (1-2)
which meets the short stitch 13-14 on Row I.
An easy way to make sure you are doing the
pattern correctly is to remember that the even
numbered rows will always start with an
extra, long stitch and end with one.

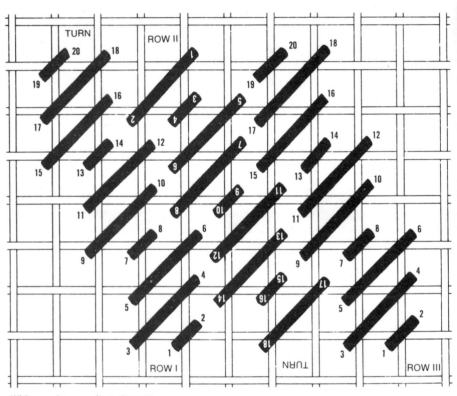

White numbers = alternate rows

52

Diagonal Cashmere Stitch

Wall panel designed by the author and worked by Rhoda Rothman. Background in the upper right area was worked in Diagonal Cashmere with the canvas turned sideways. Rows were worked upward from the righthand edge. Background at the left was done in Byzantine. Foreground is in Horizontal Scotch Stitch and figures are done in Smyrna Cross, Milanese, Horizontal Cashmere, Rice, Continental, and Diagonal Mosaic Stitches, with Gobelin for the legs and French Knots for the hair.

HORIZONTAL SCOTCH STITCH

Pillow by Charlotte Schloss. Horizontal Scotch Stitch in the center with other panels done in Milanese, Smyrna Cross, Tramé Cross, Diagonal Cashmere, and Rice Stitches.

The Horizontal Scotch Stitch has a basic unit of five slanted stitches forming a square. This pattern covers a larger area than either the Horizontal Mosaic or the Horizontal Cashmere. Like them, the Scotch is worked in rows going across the canvas from right to left. Use three strands of wool on 10-mesh canvas and turn the canvas upside down to begin each new row. For a striped effect in different colors, each row can be worked from right to left without turning the canvas. Horizontal Scotch is effective for straight borders and for filling medium to large areas of a square or rectangular shape.

Horizontal Scotch Stitch

White numbers = alternate rows

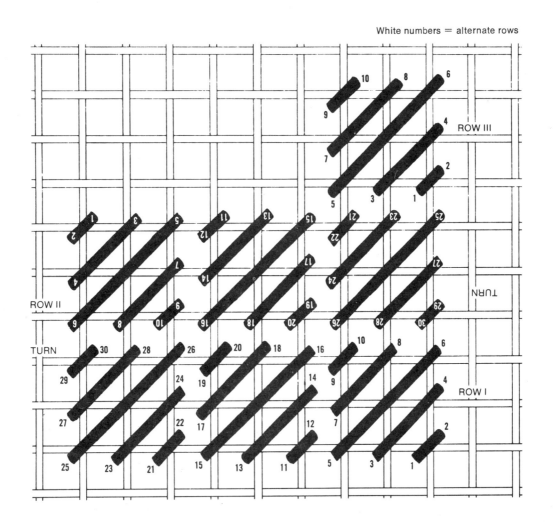

55

DIAGONAL SCOTCH STITCH

The Diagonal Scotch is no different in appearance than the Horizontal version. Instead of merging the separate units of short and long stitches into overlapping units in the diagonal version, as the Mosaic and the Cashmere do, the Scotch repeats its basic five stitches as separate units in the diagonal rows as well as in the horizontal ones. Working the Scotch pattern in diagonal rows is better for obtaining a checkerboard effect in two colors, for filling a slanted area, or for making a zigzag line.

Use three strands of wool on 10-mesh canvas and work the diagonal rows up and down without turning the canvas. Work the longest row first as in the diagram. Carry the needle under the canvas from point 30 on Row I to point 1 on Row II to continue in the same color. For a checkerboard effect, work the alternate rows in different colors, starting each row as in Row I. Between each unit of five stitches the needle is in a horizontal position under two threads when working up the canvas; it is in a vertical position under two threads when working down the canvas. The Scotch is a large stitch and covers space quickly.

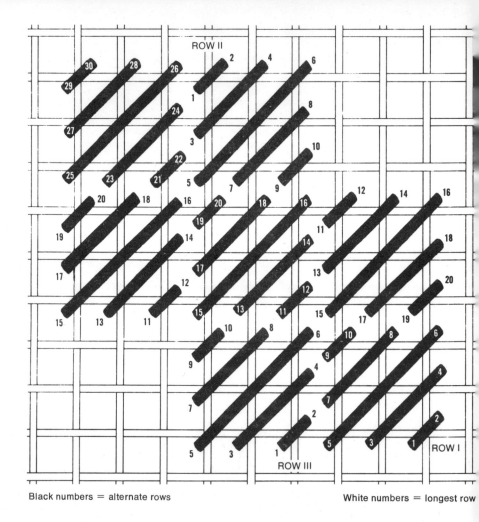

Black numbers = alternate rows

White numbers = longest row

56

Designed by the author and worked by Ruth Greer in Horizontal and Diagonal Scotch Stitches.

Diagonal Scotch Stitch

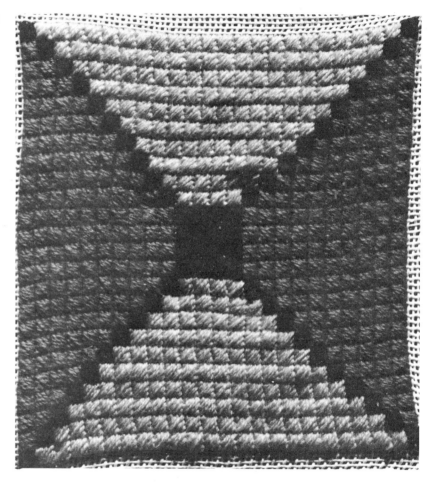

CHECKER STITCH

The Checker Stitch is a variation of the
Diagonal Scotch Stitch. Use three strands of
wool on 10-mesh canvas. Work the Diagonal
Scotch on every other row and fill in the
alternate rows with the Continental Stitch. This
makes a good background and can be used
as a large filler stitch for square areas. The
Checker Stitch also looks pretty done in
rug wool on 5-mesh canvas.

Checker Stitch

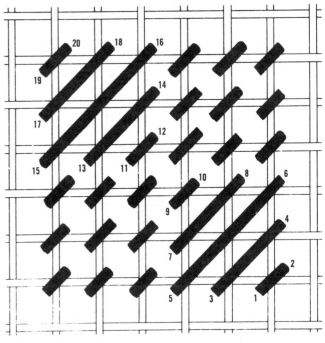

Black numbers = alternate rows

58

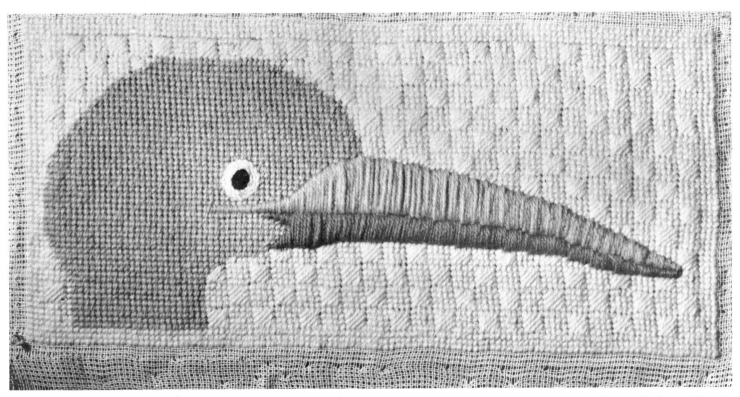

Wall panel by Jean Kummel. Background done in Checker Stitch with bird in Half Cross, Chain and Satin Stitches. Rug wool on 5-mesh canvas.

DIAGONAL STITCH

The Diagonal Stitch is based on the Scotch
Stitch and is done in units of five slanted
stitches of increasing and decreasing lengths.
However, the pattern begins with a larger
stitch than in the Scotch and the units merge,
with the fifth stitch of each unit serving as the
first stitch in the following unit. Use three
strands of wool on 10-mesh canvas and work in
diagonal rows, placing the longest row on the
canvas first. Fill in the shorter rows, working
each one from the bottom up. Note that each
short stitch must have a long one placed
next to it on the subsequent row. The Diagonal
Stitch is a good background stitch as well
as a filler stitch for large areas where a very
slanted stitch is required.

Diagonal Stitch

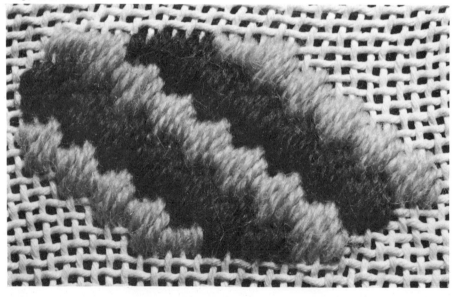

Black numbers = alternate rows

White numbers = longest row

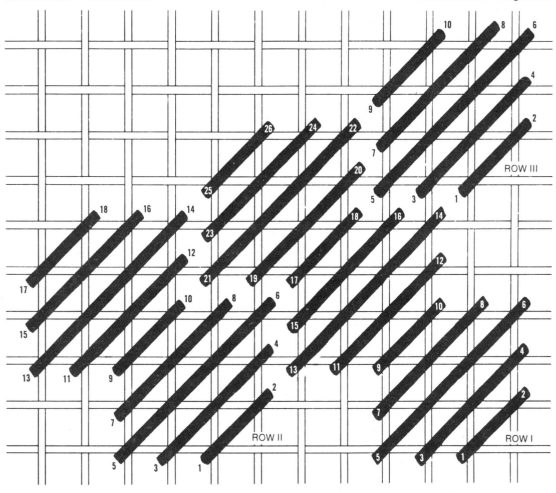

61

MILANESE STITCH

The Milanese Stitch has a basic unit of four slanted stitches increasing in size. The units are worked in diagonal rows using three strands of wool on 10-mesh canvas. Start the second row to the right or the left of the first, longest row. The points of the triangular shapes formed by the stitches should face away from each other on alternate rows.

This is a very large, decorative stitch and looks well done in two colors as part of the design or as a very slanty, textured background stitch in one color. The Milanese snags easily, so do not use it on any needleworked objects that will receive a lot of wear.

Design by Carole Widder, done in Milanese Stitch in three colors.

Wall panel by Jean Kummel. Cardinal done in Milanese, Half Cross, and Satin Stitches in rug wool on 5-mesh canvas, with Gobelin border.

Pillow by Rhoda Rothman. Done in Milanese, Gobelin, and backstitches. To obtain rows of Milanese slanting in different directions, turn canvas.

Milanese Stitch

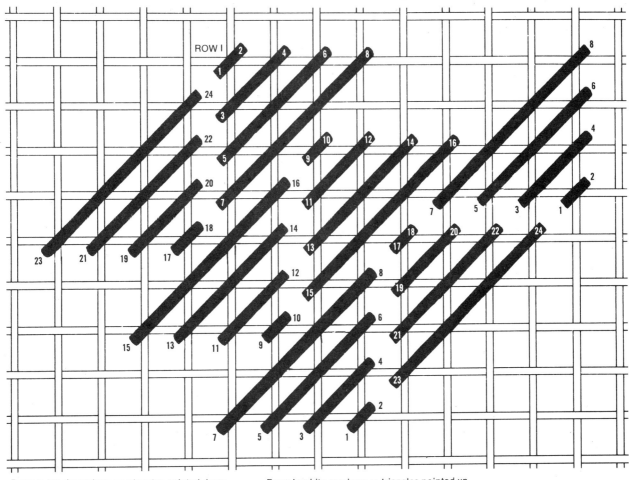

ROW I

Rows in black numbers = triangles pointed down   Rows in white numbers = triangles pointed up

63

BYZANTINE STITCH

The Byzantine Stitch gives the effect of a
jagged, diagonal line similar to the Diagonal
Stitch, but it is different in two respects.
Its slanted stitches are of equal length and
they are worked, in groups of four, by
alternately moving horizontally and vertically
in a zigzag line rather than in a pure
diagonal row.

Start the first zigzag row at the upper left of
the design area and work down to the lower
right. Once the first row is complete the
others can be worked either up or down the
canvas. The Byzantine can be worked over two
vertical and two horizontal threads of the
canvas, as shown in the diagram, or over three
or four vertical and horizontal threads of
canvas, depending on the size of the space to
be filled. Use three strands of wool on 10-mesh
canvas. This stitch produces a very striking
pattern that is shown to its best advantage
when done in two colors.

Byzantine Stitch

Sampler by Rhoda Rothman. Strong zigzag lines of
the Byzantine Stitch stand out. Striking patterns
on the outside edges are done in Bargello. Other
Stitches are: Scotch, Gobelin, Smyrna Cross, Rice,
Algerian Eye, Brick, Diagonal Mosaic, Diagonal
and Horizontal Cashmere, Plaited Gobelin,
Encroaching Oblique, Double Leviathan, Triple
Leviathan, Triangle, Leaf, Rococo, Web, Milanese,
Kalem, and Continental.

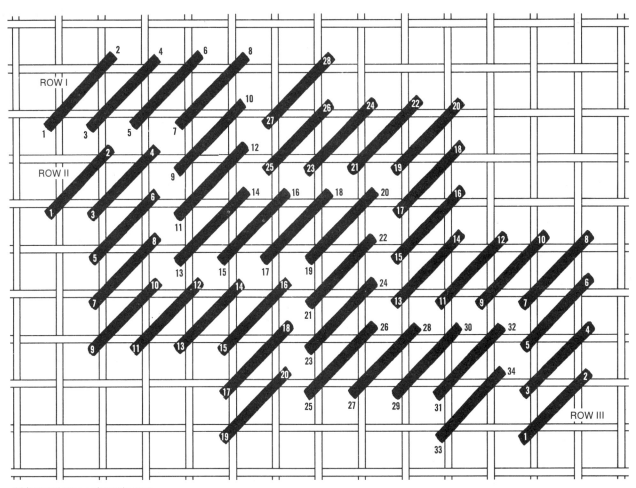

ROW I

ROW II

ROW III

White numbers = alternate rows

65

BARGELLO STITCH (Pattern Row)

Worked in zigzag, horizontal rows, Bargello consists of vertical stitches placed next to each other so that each successive stitch extends beyond the previous one as the stitches move up and then down the canvas. The successive stitches thus form peaks and valleys across the canvas. The first row is the pattern row and, once it is established, the identical arrangement of stitches is repeated for each subsequent row, either in the same color or in a different color. Bargello is worked on 14-mesh canvas in three strands of wool.

There is no set arrangement of stitches you must follow for the pattern row. By varying any or all of three factors, you can create an infinite variety of designs. The first variable factor is the length of the vertical stitch, determined by the number of horizontal threads covered by the yarn. Though the stitches within the pattern are usually of equal length, you can choose to cover anywhere from two to twelve horizontal threads. Varying the stitch length within the pattern calls for careful planning and constant counting of threads, so it is not recommended for the inexperienced worker.

The second factor that can be varied, not only from pattern to pattern but also within the same pattern, is the progression of the successive stitches up or down the canvas. This depends on how many horizontal threads one stitch extends beyond another. In Diagrams A and B, for example, each stitch covers four horizontal threads. In Diagram A, each successive stitch extends one thread beyond the previous one. In Diagram B, each successive stitch extends two threads beyond the previous one. Going up the canvas, the extension is always above the previous stitch. Going down the canvas, the extension is always below the previous stitch.

The only rule governing the extension of one stitch beyond another is that the two stitches must be side by side for at least one horizontal thread. (If all the stitches are four threads long, the most one can extend beyond the other is three threads. If the stitches are five threads long, the maximum extension possible is four threads.) The farther the stitches extend beyond each other (Diagram B), the greater the peaked effect. The less the stitches extend beyond each other, the more scalloped the effect. Two or more stitches may be placed next to each other for their entire length before a stitch is advanced up or down the canvas (Diagram C). This treatment results in a still more scalloped effect or in some cases a boxed one (see page 68).

In the pattern shown in the photograph and in Diagram D, each stitch goes over five threads. However, the number of threads each stitch extends beyond the previous one varies, so that the total effect is a combination of peaks and scallops.

To place the pattern row properly, first fold the canvas in half, making a central vertical line from the top of the canvas to the bottom. Count 26 threads up from the bottom of the canvas along this center line and begin stitch 1-2 at that point on the center line. (This leaves a 1-inch margin at the bottom of the canvas and enough room for the pattern row to go down the canvas.) From the center line, follow the numbers in the diagram and work the stitches shown so they form a row across to the left side of the canvas. Repeat the sequence as often as necessary. After you have worked stitch 69-70, for instance, begin the sequence again with stitch 3-4. (Stitch 1-2 is not repeated.) When you have worked across to the left side of the canvas, return to the center line and work the same pattern in reverse (beginning with stitch 67-68 and working back to stitch 1-2) across to the right edge of the canvas. Once you have this pattern row placed, you merely repeat it by working identical rows back and forth across the canvas. Always begin each stitch of the new row in the mesh hole occupied by the top of the stitch on the row below and carry the wool over the five threads directly above it. After working a row in one direction (left to right, for example), always work the next row in the opposite direction.

Vary the colors used for the successive rows. As shown in the photograph, the rows of the finished Bargello were worked in three colors. If you consider the darkest color the pattern row, you can see that the two rows above it are in a light color, and these are followed by three rows in a medium color and one in the light color. The rows below the dark one are filled in with the same arrangement of stitches and colors to complete the canvas.

DIAGRAM A

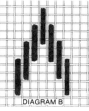

DIAGRAM B

DIAGRAM C

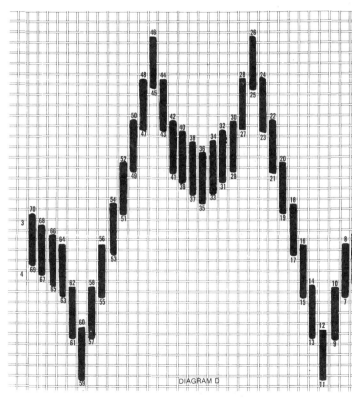

DIAGRAM D

Letters A-B = first stitch

Vertical center line of canvas

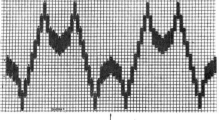

Part of Bargello pillow designed by the author and worked by Judy Walzer.

left edge of canvas

right edge of canvas

Vertical center line of canvas

BARGELLO STITCH (Pattern Outline)

The Bargello diagrammed here is based on a pattern outline instead of on one pattern row. The principles are exactly the same as for the Bargello pattern on page 66, with the stitches moving up and down the canvas in an orderly progression. Here each stitch covers four horizontal threads. Also, from two to four stitches are placed side by side before the next stitch is advanced; and in each case the stitches that advance are extended beyond the previous ones by two horizontal threads.

To work this pattern, fold the canvas in half making a vertical line down the center and mark the line with a pencil. Starting at this center line, count up enough threads to leave a 1-inch margin at the bottom of the canvas and begin Row I with stitch 1-2. Place this stitch two mesh openings to the right of the vertical center line, as in diagram. (Use three strands of wool on 14-mesh canvas.) Note that stitches 1-2 to 25-26 go up the canvas to a peak. Stitches 27-28 to 41-42 go down the canvas to a valley formed by stitches 43-44 to 49-50. Repeat these stitches in sequence across the canvas to the left-hand edge, ending in a peak stitch (in the diagram this is stitch 67-68). Return to the beginning of the row on the center line and work the same pattern of peaks and valleys across to the right edge of the canvas; but do not repeat the four valley stitches (stitches 1-2 to 7-8) already in place. End this first row at the right edge with a peak stitch.

Begin Row II at the left edge of the canvas

in the same mesh hole as the top of the peak stitch ending Row I. Note that in Row II stitches 1-2 to 17-18 move up the canvas to a plateau of four stitches (19-20 to 25-26) and stitches 27-28 to 41-42 move down to a valley (stitch 43-44). Repeating this arrangement of plateaus and valleys, work Row II all the way across the canvas to the right edge where Row I ends in a peak stitch. For Row III, repeat Row I, but note that the plateau stitches of Row II now form the valley stitches of Row III and are not repeated.

These three rows form the basic pattern outline of large and small diamonds. For placing more outline rows on the canvas, you would repeat Row II for every even-numbered row, and every odd-numbered row would repeat Row III. After the pattern outlines are placed, it is easy to fill in the spaces left with vertical stitches that follow the pattern.

In a case where you have precise dimensions to cover and you want to be sure the design will be centered horizontally as well as vertically, you can fold the canvas into quarters and begin Row I in the exact center of the canvas.

Section of belt worked in Bargello by Carole Widder.

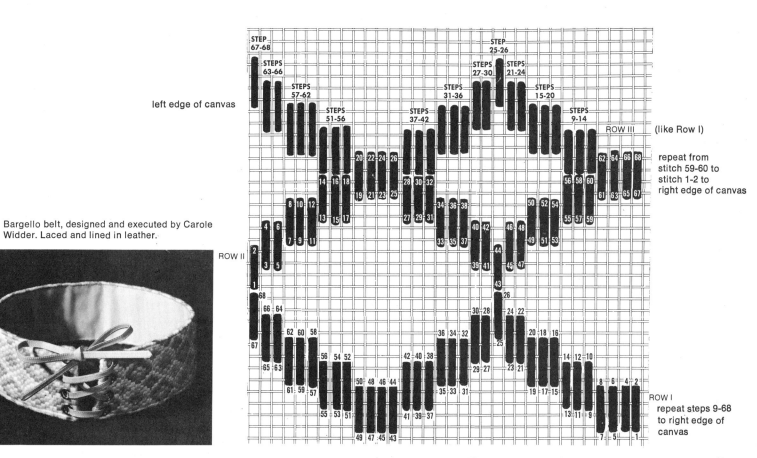

left edge of canvas

Bargello belt, designed and executed by Carole Widder. Laced and lined in leather.

ROW II

ROW I
repeat steps 9-68 to right edge of canvas

ROW III (like Row I)

repeat from stitch 59-60 to stitch 1-2 to right edge of canvas

Vertical center line of canvas

BRICK STITCH

The Brick Stitch is a vertical stitch worked in steps like the Bargello, but the stitches move up and down the canvas in a set pattern, forming horizontal rows of small zigzags. Each stitch goes over four horizontal threads of the canvas and the needle goes under two threads to make the next stitch. Going under the canvas, the needle is alternately pointed down for one stitch and up for the next stitch, producing the zigzag along the row. The next row is worked back across the canvas in the opposite direction according to the same pattern.

Use three strands of wool on 14-mesh canvas or six strands on 10-mesh canvas. The length of the stitch can be shortened for use in a small space by working the pattern over two horizontal threads and under one thread. The Brick Stitch gives a woven appearance and makes a good background. It can be worked in one or more colors.

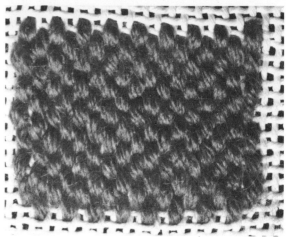

Brick Stitch

Wall panel designed by the author and worked by Joan Wallach. Background is in Brick Stitches with birds and flowers done in Continental and Cross Stitches.

Black numbers = first row   White numbers = second row

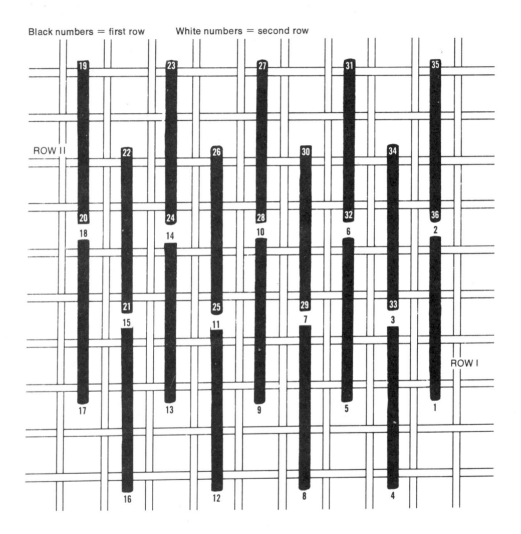

HUNGARIAN STITCH

The Hungarian Stitch is a combination of a
small Bargello and Hungarian Point (page 74).
It is worked in three strands of wool on 14-mesh
canvas. If you work it on 10-mesh canvas,
use six strands of wool.

First make a row of Bargello stitches forming
a series of V-shapes across the design area.
These stitches are of equal size. They go over
four horizontal threads and move down the
canvas one step (thread) at a time, then move
back up the same way to form the V-shapes. A
simple method of positioning the first row
correctly is to bring the needle under five
horizontal threads when going down the canvas
and under three horizontal threads when going
up the canvas.

Next, work the Hungarian Point stitches
directly above the first row of Bargello as in the
diagram. Hungarian Point consists of short
and long vertical stitches arranged in groups of
three along a horizontal row. Each group is
separated by a space. The next row of Bargello
stitches will fill in the spaces on the row of
Hungarian Point. It will also have the V-shapes
inverted so the points meet those on the
first row (see photograph).

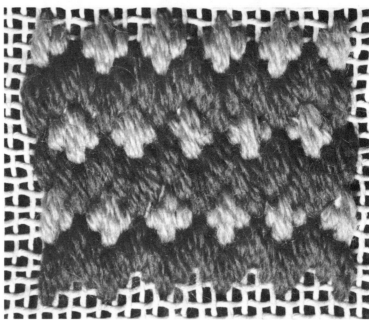

Hungarian Stitch

Black numbers = Bargello Stitches   White numbers = Hungarian Point Stitches

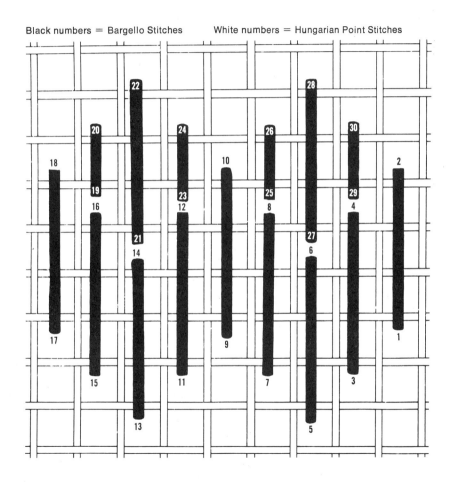

HUNGARIAN POINT

Hungarian Point is a series of short and long vertical stitches arranged in groups of three and worked in horizontal rows across the canvas. Each group (one short, one long, one short stitch) forms a small diamond shape, and one mesh space is skipped between each group on the row. The rows are worked back and forth across the canvas in three strands of wool on 14-mesh canvas or in six strands on 10-mesh canvas.

The diagram given here shows the steps for making all the rows in one color. However, it is just as simple to do the stitches in two colors, alternating colors for each row, which makes an especially pretty pattern. Work Row I as in the diagram and proceed from point 12 to point 29 on Row III with the threaded needle. Work Row III in diagram from left to right. Then work Row II in the alternate color, starting with stitch 13-14. Fill in the stitches labeled A-B with the appropriate color after you have worked the horizontal rows. The Hungarian Point is a good filler stitch in design areas and also makes a good decoration by itself for small objects like eyeglass cases and belts.

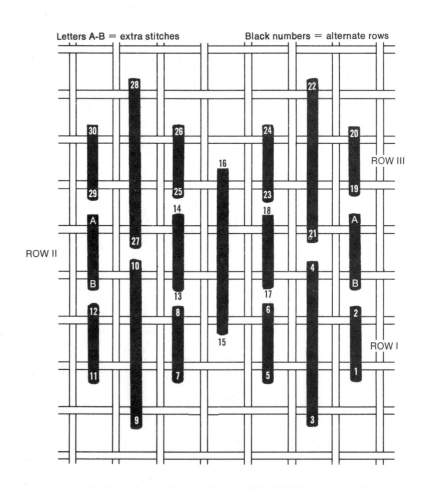

Designed by the author; worked by Ruth Greer in
Hungarian Point, Algerian Eye, Diagonal Mosaic,
Kalem and Tent Stitches. Fish motif can be used as
a repeat pattern or enlarged. Hungarian Point was
worked with the canvas turned sideways.

PARISIAN STITCH

The Parisian Stitch consists of alternating short and long vertical stitches worked continuously across the canvas in horizontal rows. Unlike the Hungarian Point, which it resembles, it does not have the short and long stitches separated into groups. Starting at the right-hand corner, work the rows back and forth as in the diagram. Use three strands of wool on 14-mesh canvas or six strands on 10-mesh canvas.

The pattern is most effective when done in two colors. This can be worked by repeating each color on alternate rows or by first working all the large stitches in one color and then working all the small stitches in another color. The pattern has a nice woven appearance and in certain colors looks like some American Indian decorations. To maintain the pattern and make sure the short stitches are placed above the long stitches (and the long ones above the short ones) on each succeeding row, it is best to work back and forth even when using a different color on alternate rows, though in that case you can reverse steps 13 and 14 to begin the alternate rows.

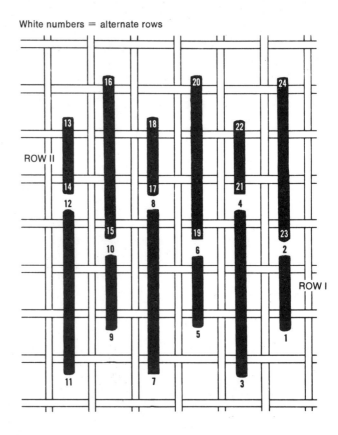

White numbers = alternate rows

ROW II

ROW I

Parisian Stitch worked in two colors.

Parisian Stitch worked with all the large stitches in one color and all the small stitches in another color.

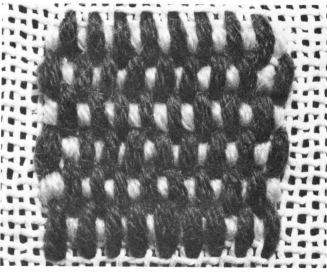

TRIANGLE STITCH

The Triangle Stitch is one of several decorative patterns that is formed by a symmetrical arrangement of a rather large number of stitches in a specific space. Previous examples were the Double Leviathan (formed of Cross Stitches) and the Triple Leviathan Stitch (formed of slanted stitches). The Triangle Stitch is formed of vertical stitches in varying lengths. It is a very large, geometric stitch and looks best as part of a geometric design (either in the corners of the design or in the center of it). It can also be used as a checkerboard pattern. Use three strands of wool on 14-mesh canvas or six strands on 10-mesh canvas. Follow the numbers on the diagram and turn the canvas clockwise as you work. The Cross Stitches in the corners can be put in as you go along.

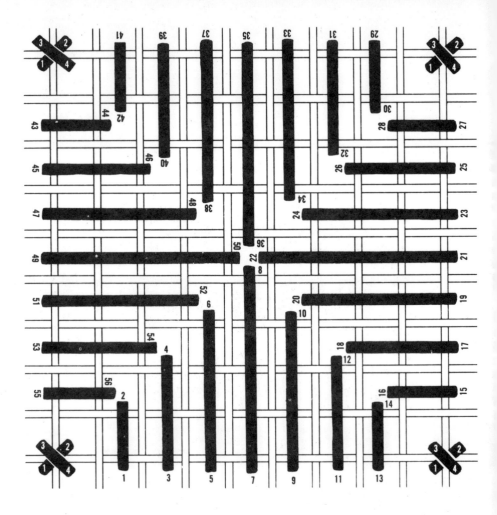

Designed and worked by Carole Widder in Triangle and Horizontal Mosaic Stitches with bands of Continental Stitches.

Triangle Stitch

ALGERIAN EYE STITCH

The Algerian Eye is a smaller geometric design than the Triangle Stitch and lends itself more readily to being worked in rows. It consists of a combination of slanted, vertical and horizontal stitches. Each stitch is worked inward to the central mesh as shown in the diagram. Place the stitches in the order given, remembering to return to the center to begin each new stitch. You can use three strands of wool on 10-mesh canvas, but this pattern looks better in six strands on 5-mesh penelope canvas. Keep the stitches a bit taut.

To work the pattern in a horizontal row, carry the yarn under the canvas from the center of the completed Algerian Eye to point 1 at the right of it. To work the pattern in a diagonal row, return from the center to point 12 on the rear of the canvas and slide the needle through the back of completed stitches 11, 10, 9, and 8 before you proceed to point 1 diagonally below. Working in diagonal rows, you can achieve a checkerboard effect, beginning the alternate color as shown in the diagram. Backstitches can be added between the horizontal rows of the pattern. Used in a large design on 10-mesh canvas, one complete Stitch can serve as an eye for birds, fish or animals; and separate, complete Stitches can be used for windows on houses.

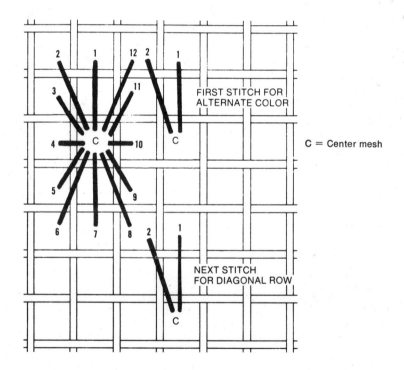

FIRST STITCH FOR ALTERNATE COLOR

C = Center mesh

NEXT STITCH FOR DIAGONAL ROW

Design by Judy Walzer, done in Algerian Eye
worked in diagonal rows using four colors.
Backstitches are placed between horizontal rows.

LEAF STITCH

The Leaf Stitch uses a series of slanted stitches of equal length, plus one shorter vertical stitch, to form a leaf shape. Work it in three strands of wool on 10-mesh canvas and follow the diagram. Since this is a large design stitch, it can be used only in large areas. The shape used separately is ideal for working individual leaves, for detailing wings on birds, and for making small trees. Grouped together, the leaf shapes are good for large trees. If desired, a row of backstitches can be placed down the center of each leaf shape.

Leaf Stitch

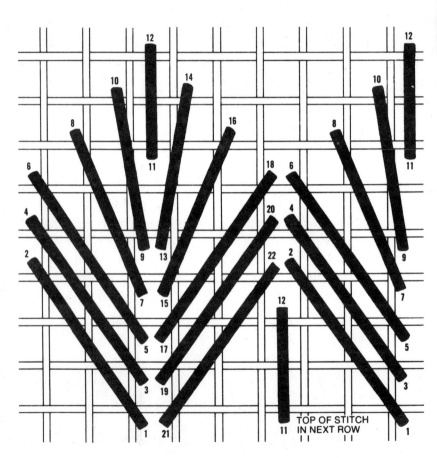

TOP OF STITCH
IN NEXT ROW

Designed by the author and worked by Frances Aronoff. The tree top is formed of Leaf Stitches with Knotted Stitches for the trunk. Note that one Leaf Stitch is equal in height to two and one-half rows of the Encroaching Gobelin Stitches in the background. (Each row of Gobelin was worked over four threads.)

Wall panel designed by author. The owl's wings are worked entirely in Leaf Stitches and the rest of the body is done in Bargello. Bird's face is in Smyrna Cross, Slanted Gobelin, Continental, and Algerian Eye Stitches. Beak is of Satin Stitches. Background is in Diagonal Mosaic, Diagonal Cashmere, and Continental Stitches.

KALEM STITCH

The Kalem Stitch and the eight Stitches described on the following pages all consist of slanted stitches worked in alternate directions. In the Kalem, the stitches are slanted one way going up the canvas and slanted the opposite way going down the canvas. Worked in vertical rows, the stitches converge to form V-shaped stripes. This gives a pretty ribbed effect that can be used for a textured background. The rows of small V-shapes are also good for leaves, fish gills and tree trunks. Use three strands of wool on 10-mesh canvas. While following the diagram, note that you begin and end each vertical row with a small, slanted stitch as you work up and down the canvas. The other stitches are all equal to each other in length.

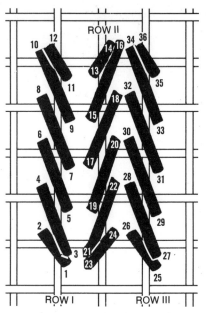

Black numbers = stitches slanted to upper left
White numbers = stitches slanted to upper right

84

Kalem Stitch

STEM STITCH

The Stem Stitch uses larger slanted stitches than the Kalem, but it is also worked in vertical rows, with the stitches first slanted one way and then in the opposite way so they converge. Follow the numbers in the diagram, working down the canvas and then back up. Use three strands of wool on 10-mesh canvas or six strands on 5-mesh canvas. You can also put a line of backstitches (see page 38) in between the stitches that converge to form the V-shapes. This stitch looks well combined with the Long Arm Cross (page 96) or by itself as a textured background. Use it in designs wherever ribbed lines are called for.

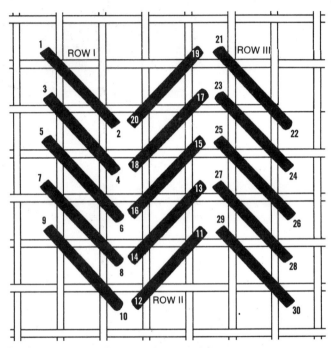

Black numbers = stitches slanted to upper left
White numbers = stitches slanted to upper right

Stem Stitch

Wall panel, "Split Face," designed by the author and worked by Frances Aronoff. Stem Stitches form the neck. Other Stitches used are: Gobelin, Diagonal Mosaic, Cross, Smyrna Cross, Rice, Continental and Brick.

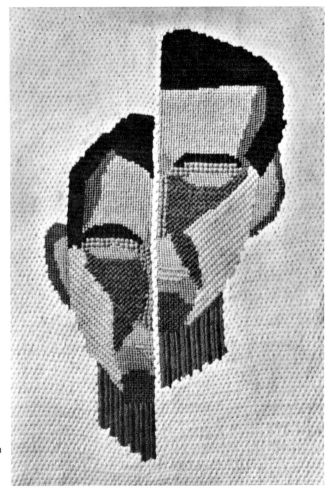

FERN STITCH

The Fern Stitch, like the Stem Stitch, consists of slanted stitches that alternate in direction. However, here the alternate stitches actually cross each other as they converge into a V-shape. Begin each new row at the top of the canvas and work down. Start each row with a Cross Stitch as shown in the diagram. Instead of working the alternate slants separately as in the Stem Stitch and the Kalem Stitch, work them together so they cross as you move down the canvas. Use three strands of wool on 10-mesh canvas. The Fern Stitch makes a very thick, braided-looking line. It also gives a nice ribbed effect as a filler stitch and can fit into small or medium-sized areas.

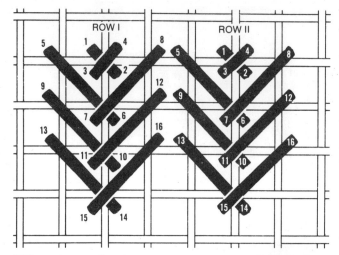

White numbers = alternate rows

Fern Stitch

88

Pillow by Jean Kummel. Stems of flowers done in
Fern Stitches. Body of small cat done in Kalem
Stitches (with canvas turned sideways). Body of
large cat in Byzantine Stitches. Background is in
Continental, Crewel, and Fern Stitches.

HERRINGBONE STITCH

In the Herringbone Stitch, the slanted stitches alternate in direction and are crossed at the bottom of each resulting V-shape as in the Fern Stitch. But in addition each new V-shape also overlaps the top of the V-shape to its left. To do this, the Herringbone is worked in horizontal rows from left to right. Follow the steps in the diagram. Use three strands of wool on 10-mesh canvas. It is easier to work these stitches on penelope canvas, but mono-canvas can be used if you are careful not to let the stitches slip. The completed Herringbone has a very solid, woven effect when done in one color. It is striking when done in two colors alternating with each row or two. A single row of Herringbone adds a decorative touch to a background done in another stitch.

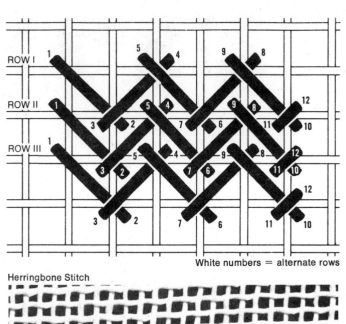

White numbers = alternate rows

Herringbone Stitch

HERRINGBONE GONE WRONG STITCH

The Herringbone Gone Wrong is the pattern that is produced when the Herringbone is worked back and forth across the canvas instead of only from left to right. Instead of having the stitches crossing in the same woven pattern on all the rows, the direction of the weave is reversed on the alternate rows. Use three strands of wool on 10-mesh canvas.

White numbers = alternate rows

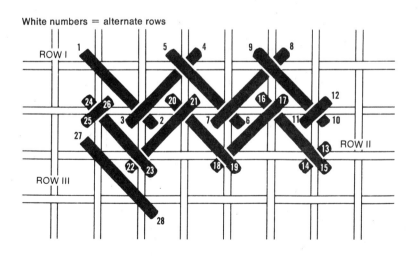

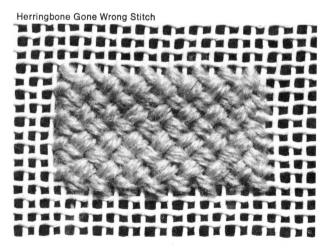

Herringbone Gone Wrong Stitch

TWO-COLOR HERRINGBONE STITCH

The Two-Color Herringbone Stitch has one row of the regular Herringbone crossed by an inverted row of Herringbone in another color. Follow the numbers in the diagram for the first color and put in the second color by following the letters. Work all the rows from left to right. Use three strands of wool on 10-mesh canvas. This stitch looks exceptionally well on 5-mesh canvas in six strands of wool for each color.

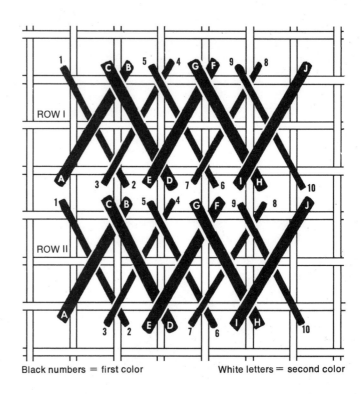

Black numbers = first color   White letters = second color

Two-Color Herringbone Stitch

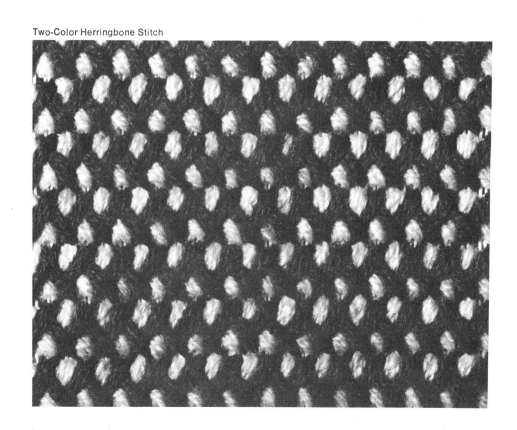

PLAITED GOBELIN STITCH

In the Plaited Gobelin, the slanted stitches of
each horizontal row are crossed by the slanted
stitches on the next horizontal row worked in
the opposite direction. Work back and forth
across the canvas as shown in the diagram. Use
six strands of wool on 10-mesh canvas. The
Plaited Gobelin does not cover very well and is
only good in very large areas, but it is very
decorative and looks woven.

Black numbers = stitches slanted to upper left
White numbers = stitches slanted to upper right

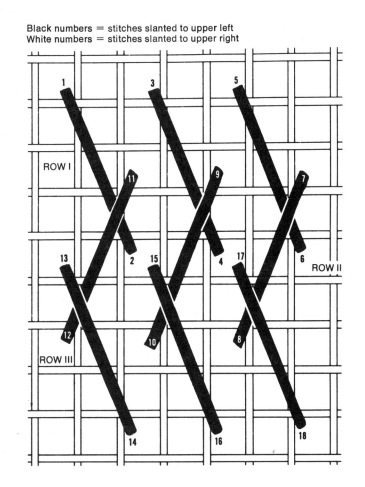

LONG ARM CROSS STITCH

The Long Arm Cross is a long, slanted stitch crossed by a shorter stitch slanted in the opposite direction and is worked in horizontal rows. Its braided effect is similar to the Plaited Gobelin, but the rows do not interlock as they do in Plaited Gobelin and the rows of Long Arm Cross form single, textured lines or heavy ribbing rather than a large weave. The Long Arm Cross is good on 10-mesh canvas using three strands of wool or on 5-mesh canvas using six strands of wool. Work back and forth across the canvas, turning it for each new row. Fill in the missing stitch at either end of each row if desired. The Long Arm Cross makes a good straight line and combines well with the Stem Stitch. On 5-mesh canvas it is an excellent rug stitch.

Long Arm Cross Stitch

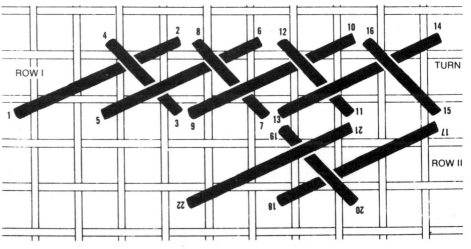

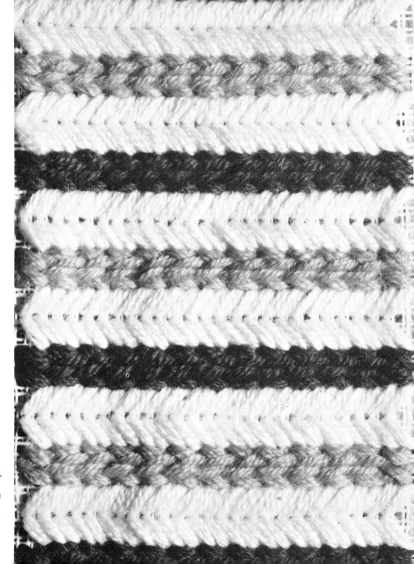

Designed by the author; worked by Ruth Greer.
Stem and Long Arm Cross Stitches on 5-mesh
canvas. (Canvas turned sideways to work Stem
Stitches.)

LONG AND SHORT OBLIQUE STITCH

The Long and Short Oblique Stitch is a long, slanted stitch crossed by a short stitch slanted in the opposite direction. These stitches are worked in vertical rows, and each long stitch is crossed before the next one is made. Long stitches on alternate rows converge.

Use three strands of wool on 10-mesh canvas. Follow the numbers in the diagram and work up and down. This is a very decorative stitch which makes a large, zigzag pattern and it should be used in large areas. It looks best in one color.

Long and Short Oblique Stitch

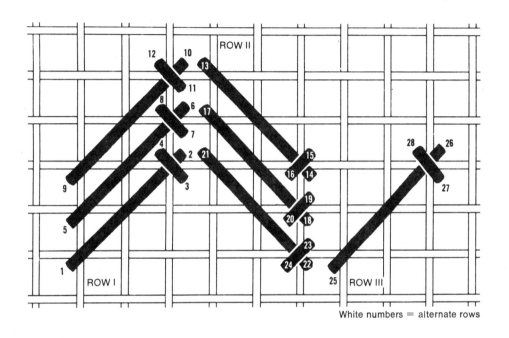

Index